DEDICATION

To my parents, who have always
supported me bigly.

www.mascotbooks.com

For more information, please contact:
Mascot Books
560 Herndon Parkway #120
Herndon, VA 20170
info@mascotbooks.com

Library of Congress Control Number: 2017905189

CPSIA Code: PBANG0717A
ISBN-13: 978-1-68401-258-9

Printed in the United States

don't be like Trump

Trump

written by David Olson

illustrations by Marie Foster

Whatever you do,
don't be like Trump.

Because President Trump
is the world's greatest grump.

He's foul and he's rude,
with a bad attitude,

and he's proven himself
to be quite a crude dude.

Trump is a
braggart,

he's boastful
and vain.

He'll say almost
anything,

just for the
fame.

You should be generous,
kind, and polite.

When you go into the world,
be humble and bright.

Trump claims to be righteous,
    it should come as no shock,

that when he's out on the golf course,
    it's all Locker Room Talk.

You should summon the courage
to not follow along,

but stand up for what's right
when you know something's wrong.

Trump's lack of good sense,
it grows like a weed,

for he's planted
around him
some
not-so-good
seeds.

You should pick friends
who choose love over hate,
who enrich and inspire,
and help you become great.

Yes, Trump is rich —

it's his great source of pride!

But what good is rich,

if you're never satisfied?

You should work hard.
You should study and learn.

You'll be much more fulfilled
by the success that you earn.

history of cheeses

And while President Trump
might not be all bad,

he's so full of himself—
it's really quite SAD!

But saddest of all?
    Trump is all kinds of mean,
when he's up late at night
    on his Twitter machine.

Trump froths and he foams
as he types his decree,
calling out those
who dare disagree.

You should have
empathy,
be thoughtful
and nice.

Before you hit
SEND
always think
twice.

Because words have power,
much more than you know.

So try to go high,

when they go low.

Keep this in mind
for when you grow up:

Whatever you do—